THEY SAW SASQUATCH

Close Encounters With Bigfoot

GARY AND WENDY SWANSON

Cover Artwork by CODY A. SIMS

Copyright © 2016 Wendy and Gary Swanson
All rights reserved.

Published by Swanson Literary Group
ISBN: 1537280074
ISBN-13: 978-1537280073

Other books by the authors:

Sasquatch Encounters: True Tales Of Bigfoot
Hiking Sasquatch Country: Tales And Trails In Bigfoot's Backyard
Hire-Education For Job Seekers

Other books by Gary Swanson:

Car Sharks and Closers: A Master Closer's Secrets Of Closing Car Deals
Close It Or Lose It: Successfully Negotiating Car Sales
The Art Of The Car Deal
Quit Smoking Or I'll Shoot

Other books by Wendy Swanson:

Diggin' Up Bones: A Genealogy Research Guide

GARY AND WENDY SWANSON

CONTENTS

- Introduction — 7
- Sasquatch And Aliens? — 9
- Rogue River Trail — 12
- Reported Bigfoot Sightings — 15
- All The Bells And Whistles — 106

GARY AND WENDY SWANSON

INTRODUCTION

There have been stories told about Sasquatch for centuries. From the abominable snowman or Yeti in the Himalayas, which has now been proven to be fact; to the Bigfoot stories all across North America that started with Native Americans and then non-Natives quickly began retelling these stories and also sharing their own experiences.

We are avid hikers, and it was due to sharing some of our adventures with people we met who had similar experiences that led us to start collecting Sasquatch stories. This book includes some recorded history of the Bigfoot in the Southern Oregon area, as well as reported experiences from folks who shared their stories with us as well as a few of own.

The encounters we have included in this book came largely from people we either know personally or because of their credible profession, which include a U.S. Forestry Service agent, two Bureau of Land Management agents, one of whom also serves as a minister on his own time, a sheriff's deputy, a doctor, a fire department employee, rural land owners, goldminers, an accredited Sasquatch hunter and hikers and rafters. Basically, people who we deem to be most trustworthy.

It is amazing just how many people have had encounters with the Bigfoot creatures, and people travel to the Pacific Northwest from all over the world to search the mountains and wilderness areas for the "big guy." Once you begin to explore our ruggedly beautiful country, you will come to realize the magnitude of why these vast and somewhat unexplored areas defy even the most adventurous to even attempt entering! There are valleys and mountains in our country that have never felt the presence of humans. So, could Bigfoot live here in anonymity? Extremely possible! Our own discoveries have changed our opinions on whether or not the Sasquatch exists, from "not possible" to certainly a "good likelihood!"

Many of these encounters were included in our book "Hiking Sasquatch Country: Tales and Trails in Bigfoot's Backyard," and the rest are additional sightings that we have gathered from those who have also had their own encounters. We have not included the few photographs that were submitted, as it seems the Sasquatch does not seem to care about giving adequate notice so people can capture it clearly, and the few shots that were submitted were among those stories that we did not include because their validity was questionable.

We love to hike, but for us, it has never been the stealthy trek of the wildlife photographer; what with panting dogs, talking, stepping on twigs, and stumbling over rocks, it is understandable that our sighting critters is usually at a distance, however our forests are home to deer, bear, wolves, coyotes, cougars, bald eagles, turkeys, hawks, owls and thousands more! They fear us more than we do them. The only cautions we can knowingly give, is do not come near a momma bear with cubs, realize that a cougar will follow you and may attack if a lone hiker is not alert, and be aware that we do have a few rattlesnakes in some places and there will be poison oak and ticks in the area.

Welcome to Bigfoot country!

SASQUATCH AND ALIENS?

When we began interviewing some of our submitters, at first we had a tendency to cast a leery glance in each other's direction when the subject went from Bigfoot to flying saucers.

The first time I ever heard of an actual sighting was back in 1970 shortly after arriving in the Pacific Northwest.

I was doing business with some fairly affluent people in Washington State. They owned a nice home with lots of acreage, and after our transaction was completed, we began to relax and get to know one another better.

The property they described sounded like paradise! Beautiful, rolling acres with open pastures surrounded by mountains, and bordered by trees that soared to the heavens! Although not far from Vancouver, it was a retreat with all the amenities, but with the nearest neighbor over a mile away, and the property bordering on a national forest area that was as unexplored and pristine as if it had never had a human set foot in it.

These nice folks were retired professionals and highly educated and prosperous. As we became closer friends while awaiting my associates to complete final delivery of our sale, they began to take me into their confidence. Obviously, they wished to share some exciting experiences that they had on their property, and they explained that they seldom told anyone of these events out of fear of being laughed at.

I have found over the years that this is a common thread

among our contributors. These experiences were so exciting to them, but they were seldom able to share them with anyone for fear of being ridiculed even though they were all so true. I guess it would be like owning a beautiful new luxury sports car and having to leave it in the garage when you were just dying to show it off!

Anyway; they could see I was interested, although somewhat skeptical, but not critical. They described occurrences, footprints of these mysterious beasts, and even so far as to sightings, and acknowledgement between them and two large Sasquatch creatures that consisted of a wave and a nod of the head from the larger of the beasts that they assumed to be a male. This truly was an exceptional discussion, and it culminated with them inviting me to visit them and see for myself!

Then came the game changer; with my ignorance of what I could have experienced had I gone ahead with a visit. They evidently felt they could trust me implicitly, and then explained about two occurrences of some sort of alien spacecraft landing on their property and of the burned areas that had been left behind. They described the strange lights at night and the charred ground remaining when they found the spots in the daylight!

Being totally unaware and skeptical at the time, I never followed through with a visit, because when they brought the UFO incident up, I incorrectly dismissed everything they had previously told me as an insane story! Had I thought this through at the time, I would have realized that two highly educated adults with backgrounds as university professors, and their soon to be very successful offspring would not all four be delusional!

Another opportunity lost due to skepticism without any basis other than human nature. Since that time so long ago, and especially since we began researching sightings for our books, I have found Sasquatch sightings and unknown spacecraft occurrences to have a somewhat common thread!

Some of our interviews have indicated that our friends who are reluctant to even discuss their initial experience have seemed to not be telling the whole story. That is, until we asked, "Is there anything else that you wish to report, such as even something as strange as a UFO?" Often, that question would generate a gasp of relief that would generate an entire new sequence of events that the folks seemed to just let it pour out; as if pressure was being released. Many of those submitters however, did not allow us to connect the two happenings; as the general consensus seems to be that asking people to believe in Bigfoot is one thing, but as one person explained, "If you throw an alien spacecraft on top of this story, they'll think I'm nuts for sure!"

This reasoning is a common denominator with some our storytellers, so for this reason, this information will have to someday stand on its own. After all, we have never seen an alien spacecraft on our day hikes, so we will stick to what seems logical and that we can believe in, because of our personal encounters and the absolute sincerity of our submitters.

GARY AND WENDY SWANSON

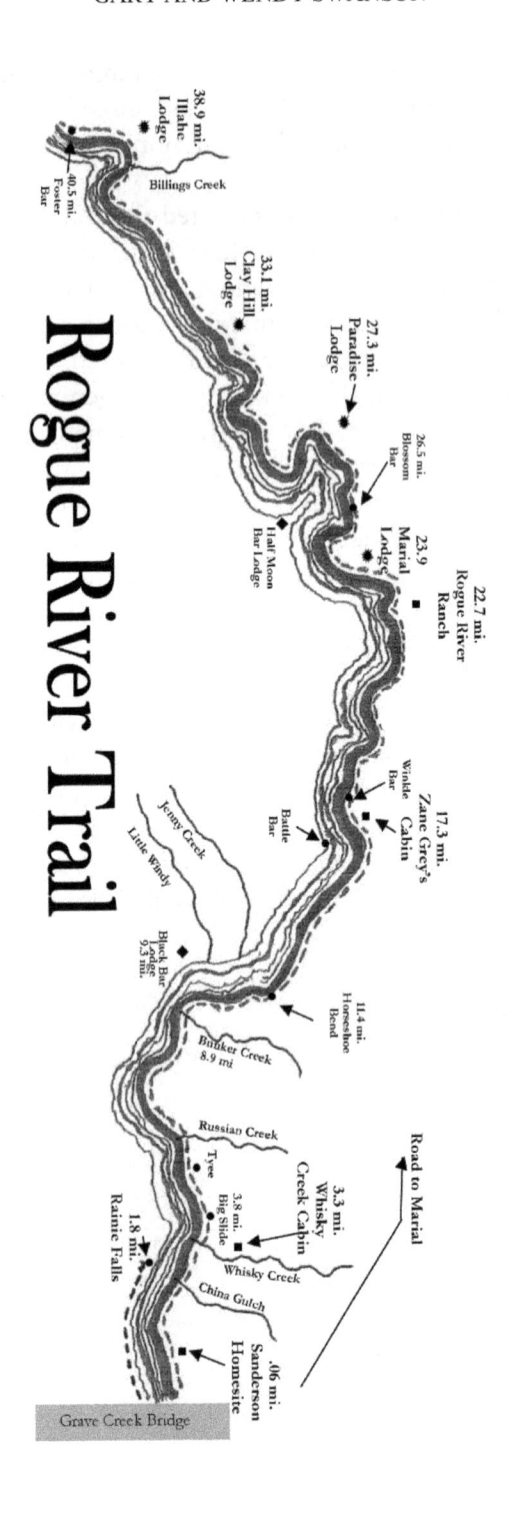

Rogue River Trail

ABOUT THE ROGUE RIVER TRAIL

We include this map as a guide for distances for hikers wishing to walk the Rogue River Trail.

Grave Creek flows into the Rogue just before the bridge, and was named because Martha Leland Crowley, a pioneer's daughter, was buried alongside the creek. Her grave is located in Sunny Valley near the Grave Creek Covered Bridge.

The Rogue River has a long history of unsolved murders throughout its violent gold mining days and Indian wars.

The curse of Black Bar: It is rumored that Black Bar on the Rogue River carries a curse! The Black Bar Lodge was named after gold miner William Black whose claim was 8.8 miles down the Rogue River from where Grave Creek enters the Rogue. William Black was murdered near where the Black Bar Lodge now sits, put into his boat and launched down the Rogue. The murder remains unsolved.

In 1998 the Black Bar Lodge was owned by Bill and Sally Hull. Mr. Hull was robbed and murdered by Josh Cain and his half-brother Trevor Walraven.

In December 2006 James Kim and his family became stranded on a logging road while attempting a drive through the back country to the Oregon coast. Mr. Kim tried a cross country trip on foot to find the lodge by GPS coordinates to obtain help. His body was found just about a mile from Black Bar. Coincidence or curse? Note: His family was found alive.

The Sasquatch murders of the Almeda Mine (an included

hike in *Hiking Sasquatch Country*) happened somewhere west of the Grave Creek Bridge.

Zane Grey, the noted author, purchased a mining claim in the 1920's, and stayed at his cabin the summer he wrote his novel, "Rogue River Feud." An avid fisherman; Grey reportedly said, "the best memories of my life, are at this place." During his stay, he uncovered the Sasquatch murders from local publications and after doing some research, he re-reported the story nationally while in Grants Pass, Oregon.

REPORTED BIGFOOT SIGHTINGS

Dear Readers,

After introducing our book *Hiking Sasquatch Country*, we were overjoyed with the sales and the response from so many readers. Many people it seems have had personal Bigfoot experiences, and as a result, they came away with a belief that the elusive creature lives among us! The requests to include actual reader stories were enough that we advertised for anyone who has had a Sasquatch happening to submit them for possible inclusion in this book, and the response has been overwhelming. We did not realize that there are so many people all across our nation who have had unexplainable occurrences involving mysterious sightings and events relating to the possibility that an apelike being exists in our more remote areas. These events are oftentimes just shared with one's close circle of friends and relatives, and after mixed responses ranging from, "Were you drunk?" to "You've been working too hard!" they never mentioned their experience anymore. Now, since we made an offer to publish some of these stories, we have received many interesting tales of reported sightings and encounters. Many of the submissions were so similar that we had to select ones that covered the important points common to all. Although we were intrigued and mystified by our own experiences with our Bigfoot brother, we had no idea that so many people out there have had similar sightings and encounters! The only reward anyone has received for sending in their story is a copy of our book, so their submissions are truly their honest effort in telling their stories only for posterity.

To protect privacy, and because we cannot guarantee the authenticity or accuracy of these stories, some are printed with the submitters initials only. We have printed them without change other than slight grammar and spelling corrections.

We would like to thank all of those who were willing to share their Sasquatch stories with us, and it is our wish that you enjoy these stories, and many of our readers will hopefully enjoy the hikes throughout our beautiful and wild Southern Oregon Sasquatch country. We hope that sometime in the near future, thanks to our new readers, that perhaps we may be publishing a book of Sasquatch photographs; so please start carrying your cameras at the ready!

The first three stories are our own possible Bigfoot encounters.

Date of occurrence
September 18, 2012

Location
Briggs Creek Trail

Our last hike on the Briggs Creek Trail was quite interesting! After a little over an hour down the trail, which runs parallel to Briggs Creek; off to our left, we heard the brush move. Assuming that we had startled a deer, we continued on, but so did the sounds of the animal moving alongside and parallel to the trail.

The terrain here is really thick with brush and thickets of thorns, blackberries, willows, and are quite impassable and high enough and thick enough to prevent seeing over five feet into the dense foliage.

Instead of their normal barking and pulling at their leashes to go in pursuit, our dogs were silently pulling hard to continue on the path and the hair was up on their backs; not their normal "see the deer" attitude.

I wasn't about to claw my way through the thorns to observe a raccoon or whatever it could be, so we continued. We kept hearing this noisy critter for about a half hour as we kept up a steady downhill pace, and although curious, I just figured it to be a young and curious fawn or something, but we were surprised at how much noise it made. The going through the brush would have been tough and it had to have been of good size to make that much noise. Also, it is highly unusual for any wild animal to follow humans! They will always move quickly away.

We knew only that it was not human, as there were no other people or vehicles at the trailhead and there had been no mining activity, and even so, a miner would have welcomed a quick visit or at least a "hello."

Farther down the trail, where it gets continually closer until it crosses over the creek to meander along the other side, the noises ceased — and just when I thought we'd finally meet our inquisitive follower!

The noises were soon forgotten as we continued our hike, and finally we reached the halfway mark for today's hike and began our return. I think that we were gone for another two hours before we returned to cross the creek again.

Having no concerns about those earlier noises, we were reminded suddenly as we heard the same rustling, this time on our right side, and realized that was the same place they stopped before! As we continued back up the trail our visitor stayed alongside again, and I now *had to* find out what it was!

After another half mile, I spotted a possible route through the place a giant tree had fallen, crushing the trees around it. Wendy holding the dogs back (and the car keys just in case), I crashed my way through the bushes with small bits of clothing and skin coming off as I traversed a downhill course toward the creek. Camera at the ready, I came to a small clearing, and peering at me over the roots of a fallen tree was a "gorilla face?" My mind reeled as I pushed the camera's button while thinking it was, "some kid in a Halloween mask!"

Well it wasn't; in fact the camera only captured the shadow, and when I took off running around the tree, there was nothing! Just the sound of something rapidly thrashing through the surrounding bushes, and whatever it was, it had run the distance from the root ball through the thick brush in just four seconds. Over 100 feet! No human could have done that!

I can't say it was …, but I sure can't say it wasn't! The face I saw in the viewfinder was the face of an ape!

Gary Swanson

Date of occurrence
June 12, 2013

Location
Grayback Mountain

One of our favorite mountains to hike is Grayback Mountain; Josephine county's highest peak. As we were hiking there in June two years ago, when it was still chilly on the mountain, we had a strange experience on the way back down the trail. We were descending along a plunging creek where we saw a huge footprint. It looked human, with very-defined toes, but it was huge! Just past that point we heard strange sounds that made us both think we were hearing a large animal tearing into its' food; similar to what you might experience at a zoo. It kind of snarled and growled.

We assumed it must be a bear, perhaps eating a deer, because of the tearing, crunching and grunting sounds coming from just over the edge of the steep ravine off to our right. Our dogs were sniffing the air and their hair was up, but they showed no other signs of concern.

I was happy to move quickly down the trail, but it was a curiosity that Gary could not resist, but it was possibly quite dangerous, so he gave me his car keys, and sent me and our dogs down the path; just in case. I turned back to watch before going around the next bend, and there he was with his camera ready, as he crept slowly to the edge of the cliff. When he was about ten feet from the edge, the noise abruptly stopped! I continued to watch as he slowly leaned out over the precipice, but soon he was back on his feet heading down the trail towards me.

He said he was confronted with a large log jam which was most likely the result of years of springtime thaws and cascading floods carrying huge logs down the mountain. He couldn't see or hear anything other than the creek jumping a series of waterfalls down the steep slope. Since he didn't hear any sounds of a bear running away, he was not curious enough to climb down the forty-foot slope to search around the log pile. I asked him what he thought it was. He didn't think it reacted like a bear would, and laughingly suggested it might have been a "Bigfoot!" Thinking back on that huge footprint with water just barely seeping into it; maybe it was? Back then, we hadn't even thought seriously about the presence of such a creature, as we had both lived in cities and large towns for most of our lives.

Wendy Swanson

Date of occurrence
May 22, 2014

Location
Waters Creek Loop Trail

The last time we took the Waters Creek Loop Trail, we had an interesting experience on the upper trail. Well before we hit one of the side ravines, we heard a crashing ahead of us, and as we ascended the trail, it wound back into a ravine, and before we rounded the corner, the sound became louder. This may have been a Sasquatch. We picture the log that we felt it cut across on and the fresh footprints of some "large toed" creature that we found clearly in the wet soil where it stepped off the log and the signs where it climbed up to the gravel bank.

Gary Swanson

Date of occurrence
1922

Location
Almeda Mine

In 1922, the Almeda mine still employed close to 250 miners, and even had a floating bridge that spanned the Rogue River.

That spring, five miners walked off the job and took off downriver in search of their own gold-strike. After two weeks of no discovery, four of them decided to return to Galice, but only one of them made it back to tell the tale of two giant ape-men attacking them and the "giant forest monsters" killing his friends.

A search party was dispatched to find the men, but mainly to stop the stories and wild tales in fear that the miners would start quitting their jobs en-masse! It took a week for the searchers to find the attack site, and they only found two of the men. They reported, "The men had been killed by a savage attack on them from some unknown animals of the forest!" The third man was never found, but part of his pants and his hat were there among some "enormous sized" footprints all around the men's bodies! The party returned to the mine with the dead men's packs and the Almeda mine foreman demanded they keep quiet about their grisly discovery, or "lose their jobs." He feared that the other workers would all quit out of fear of being attacked!

The lone survivor soon disappeared, and the story was never released until the famous author Zane Grey uncovered the story and wrote about it in an Oregon Trail Magazine article. Zane Grey owned a cabin about 20 miles down the Rogue River from the Almeda, and that's where he wrote his novel, "Rogue River Feud." We hope this story adds a little intrigue to your hike? It did to ours!

Date of occurrence	Location
1986	Almeda Mine

Dear Sir:

I am answering your ad for a request for Bigfoot stories. I have one that you may not even believe, but I'll tell it anyway. In 1986, my old hunting buddy Jay and I decided to make a last hunt for deer and had planned to hunt on the area across the Rogue River where the old Almeda mine was. We couldn't figure out how to read the maps well enough to drive to the other side, so we left my old pickup at a parking place near the (Rand) ranger station and dragged my partner's drift boat down the slope; and with our gear and rifles inside, we paddled it across. By the time we angled it to the far shore, we were down river from the old Almeda site, but we pulled ashore, covered the boat with brush, and padlocked it to a large tree with a chain before we set off along the shore to the Almeda road. This is a road that winds up behind and over the top of the lower entrance. The road climbed steadily and wound around by old abandoned machinery; could have been smelters, crushers, or whatever, and we were on the old road that ran alongside the cliff overlooking the Rogue for about an hour or so, and then we spotted another road that went back across the cliff face; so we took it.

After a while, we walked past an upper entrance to the old mine, so evidently it had three different levels. Anyway, past that a ways, we finally hit a fairly flat area off an animal trail that had a small stream running down through what was almost like a real pretty meadow with a bunch of downed trees. We set up our camp on a flat area and hacked off some pine branches to lay over a sleeping area and made a shelter with a canvas tarpaulin lean-to; with pine boughs leaning against the open part, and with an open area for the smoke from our fire to escape. We were half-dead frozen by the time the fire finally started to dry things out, because it had rained hard for the past week, but now, with a good supply of firewood from a monstrous old log, we were tolerably comfortable.

This hunt was more a reminiscence of our past forty years of friendship than a real hunting trip, because Jay's doctor had given him the long face, so we knew this would be our last hunt together.

The next morning, we grudgingly rolled out to rekindle our blaze from the stack of kindling that had dried near the fire from the night before, and leisurely enjoyed our morning coffee and a few bites of hardtack. Taking our time, we put out our fire, uncased and loaded our rifles, and set out along a major animal trail that angled gradually downward toward the same direction where we had come the day before, but much higher on the mountain.

We walked a fair piece, then picked stands a ways away from each other, but within sight, and several hours passed without so much as a rabbit going by. A couple of crows told the world they had seen us, but no other creatures. We finally looked at each other and signaled to move farther down the mountain. We spent the rest of the day walking ridges and scouting trails. There was plenty of sign that deer were around, but they weren't obviously moving about, so about three in the afternoon we turned back towards camp.

It gets dark early in the mountains, so we trudged back up the trail. When we were probably a half mile from camp, we heard what sounded like a loud scream, but a combination of a roar and a screech, which we could only imagine might be a cougar, so we checked our rifles thinking to maybe get a lucky chance after all. Suddenly, a pair of does came pounding down the hill and we just barely got off the trail, or they would have run right over us in their panic! As we rounded the next corner, we saw a piece of our tarp go flying across the trail, followed by one of our knapsacks; and all of a sudden we were face to face with a huge creature!

My first thought was that it was a grizzled old miner (there are still a few left that live off the grid), but this being was more like a flat-faced bear, but much bigger. It was slouched and had huge paws and feet, and shaggy dark brown, almost black hair, and a big, wide nose. Before we could even speak, this thing picked up a large piece of log about five feet long and threw it directly at me! I turned to duck and ran smack into Jay, and we tumbled together down the slope; our rifles and caps flying, and we both went head over heels down the mountain. I crashed into a patch of brush and Jay ended up on his back, feet sticking up over a deadfall.

My mind returned to the present and I quickly climbed to my feet fearing an attack, and scrambled toward my rifle that was about ten feet up from me; and I grabbed it and prepared to defend myself, but whatever it was had gone the other way. I heard a few "thumps" in its direction, but then nothing. I looked around, and Jay was climbing over the fallen log, and we acknowledged each other by a quick, cautious wave in case the creature came back! Jay's rifle had suffered the worst. He had a scoped, bolt action, and the scope had been smashed and the stock split. My own lever action Winchester had been scratched and bruised, but the bore was clear as I quickly readied it to defend our lives, but we were alone!

We returned to the remnants of our camp, found one piece of tarp, but the coffee pot was smashed and the contents of our knapsacks were strewn down the slope, so we were lucky to find a couple of candy bars and one canteen of water. It was getting dark now, so we hurriedly got a fire going and spent a cold, watchful night.

The next morning, we limped down to the boat and made it back; so glad to be alive. I ended up with scratches and bruises, but poor Jay had two cracked ribs and a fractured wrist and broken thumb. The whole time on the long return trip we talked about the miners that were killed near the Almeda mine and wondered if our assailant was a descendent of those Sasquatch killers in the legends of those old stories from the 1920's.

Jay and I only told our story to a few friends, as we had a reputation for being hard drinkers, and Jay especially, was afraid of being laughed at. Now, I am along enough in years that I no longer care, so when I saw your ad, I figured, "What the hell!"

Bob A.   Grants Pass, OR

Date of occurrence
1990

Location
Rogue River, OR

My husband and I live on property outside of Rogue River City, where we raised 11 children. We had just finished building a horse corral for a new pony out of our own felled logs when he had to be out of town on business. One evening our Great Danes started barking frantically, and when I let them in the house, they were visibly shaking; at this same time our goats, peacocks and other animals were just going crazy. Since the children and I were home alone, I quickly made sure everyone was inside and locked the doors. It wasn't long before we heard something on two feet walking around our house. It would stop every few steps and make a sound that was similar to a gorilla beating its chest, and then the trees near the house started shaking like something was pushing the branches. I'm not sure how long this went on, but it seemed like a long while and we were very frightened; it seemed like whatever it was, was extremely angry. When the noises and footsteps finally stopped, the children and I took turns keeping watch out of our second story windows until morning.

When we went outside that morning, the new horse pen had been completely destroyed; every single log had been snapped into pieces, and we found the pony unharmed down in the meadow. We walked up into the woods behind the house to see if there was any sign of what our visitor had been. In the spots where the ground was soft, we found some very large footprints. About seven feet up in one of the trees we spotted what looked like hair. One of the boys climbed up the tree and brought the reddish-brown colored hair down with him. I contacted a friend of mine that had a connection with Southern Oregon University, and he agreed to take the hair sample to a biology lab they have on campus. It was determined to be actual hair from an unknown species. They were all baffled!

I had also talked to one of my neighbors about this incident. That same night she had heard several ear-piercing screams that she described as hair-raising.

Two weeks later two of my daughters had gone horseback riding up into the mountains behind our house. The horses began getting nervous and spooked before they had gotten far; as the girls started looking around to see what was bothering the horses they heard some cracking sound in some bushes. As they looked in that direction they saw a creature that was as tall as they were when sitting on their horses. They only saw a glimpse of it as it was walking away; they described it as having reddish-brown fur and a round head.

This was the last time any of us saw the creature, and I'm not sure if my husband believes our Sasquatch story, but he did see the results of what it did to our new corral.

Shortly before this incident, there was some logging going on in the mountains behind us, and I can't help but think that perhaps the logging activity disturbed and angered the creature, causing it to leave its cave or whatever it shelters in and vent its frustration on us.

Diane Johnson   Rogue River, OR

Date of occurrence
late June, 2013

Location
Near Quebec

A Canadians frightening experience near Quebec

I can tell you Bigfoot is real! I was deep in the wilderness north of Quebec when I crossed a stream, at which point, I found a very large footprint with well-defined toes, and I would judge it to have been a men's size 14, although I was really curious, it was toward dusk so I set up camp.

I thought no more of it until around 3:00 the next morning, when I heard a cracking and snapping as something was moving through the brush in a very careless fashion. I scrambled out of my tent, armed with my ancient revolver, inherited from my grandfather from his Royal Canadian Mounted Police days, which I carried more for nostalgia than effectiveness. My rifle was in its case in the tent.

As I shone my powerful lamp around the area, the terrific brightness must have been enough, because the noises moved off, and in a few minutes it was quiet again. Reentering my tent, I don't recall being able to fall asleep again, but I did, and when dawn broke, I was up and ready. I ate a cold breakfast, and taking my rifle I made a wide circle around my camp searching for some sign of what this apparently upset creature had been doing during its search.

Since this trip was not enroute to another destination and I planned to stay here for another week, I had no time frame. This camp out was a reward to me for putting up with the tremendous pressures and strain from being an upper manager in my investment firm. After a tremendously difficult year in which we had one crisis after another until we finally turned the corner to ending with a very successful financial picture, I didn't want to speak to another soul for at least a full week! So now, I find another creature who seems like my overstressed counterpart in the animal world!

I circled in an increasingly wider circle as close as I could judge, because the terrain consisted of hummocks of swamp grass that indicated a previously wet season, with thick alder brush that was like coiled springs that would leave a welt on my face, arms and any exposed areas on my body. I had chosen this place for my camp, because it was the only area raised up enough to provide dry ground for my campsite and was on a knoll about 30 meters across, and with a nice view of a deep, clear mountain lake that sat a hundred meters away, so was an easy jaunt with my inflatable rubber boat. The mosquitoes were not out in force yet, so it was pleasant.

My exploration found nothing but some flattened swamp grasses, which could have been from deer, beaver or muskrat as no actual bare ground was exposed.

When I finally cut my sleuthing short and returned to my camp, I discovered that I had been visited. My tent was leaning in one corner, my backpack had been ransacked, and it looked like something or someone had checked every item out of curiosity, but nothing was damaged! My guest had inspected everything, and some packages of snacks and cookies were strewn about and short on content, so whatever it was had helped itself to a snack, but my noisy return had evidently frightened it off. I don't pack too much gear, as I have a fiberglass tote that I pull; much like a toboggan that rides over the long grass like it would on snow.

Being that this knoll my camp was on was the only hard ground around, I searched carefully for footprints, and I found a sunken area that looked like a large heel had sunk in and the ground was almost bare clay, which revealed a set of four human-like toe prints. The print was about 50 centimeters long and the next track was about a meter away, and that was the only trace of my curious and noisy visitor.

During the next four days I heard nothing further, and I just relaxed, spent time fishing, reading, and unwinding from the pressures of my job.

On the day I packed up to leave, I cleaned my campsite to leave no trace of my presence and towed my gear on my sled by a rope across my chest. As I entered the forest path that led the final two miles to the crude road where I left my four wheel drive pickup, I took my habitual look back toward the lake and my camp.

There, in plain sight, was a large bear-like creature, the likes of which I have never seen! It was standing on two legs and was slightly stooped over, and appeared to be investigating the area. It was shaggy like a bear that has multi-colored fur in the spring, and it looked to be more similar in physical shape to a man than an animal. It did not have the bulk of the ape or the shape of an animal accustomed to walking on all fours. I scrambled for my cell phone to get a photo, but by the time I dug it out of my pack, the creature had departed, and I don't know where. It could have seen me looking at it and hidden on the other side of the knoll, but I waited another 10 minutes before giving up, as I had a long drive home.

As a professional businessman I tell you of my experience because it's one of those stories that one in my business cannot obviously afford to discuss with peers or clients, and therefore you can appreciate why I must remain anonymous, but my family will be able to see my experience in print and my kids can know what "Daddy did on his retreat!"

> Jason A., Canada

Date of occurrence	Location
June, 2009	Happy Camp, CA

Thanks for letting me tell my story. I have kept it quiet due to the fact my parents live in a small town in Northern California, and I didn't want to publicize the area to protect their privacy.

This happened in 2009 and I had just got out of the U.S. Marine Corps, and was living with my folks until my paperwork cleared and processed so I could start work as a deputy in the sheriff's department.

On this particular Sunday, I had spent time with an old friend, and when I pulled into my parents rural driveway, my mother came running up to my car with a shotgun in her hands and a strange look on her face! She didn't act scared, just shook up and out of breath. Mom thrust the Mossberg into my hands and pointed down the road to the bridge that was about a quarter mile past our driveway; she said, "There's a huge animal that came up from the creek and walked across the road and back down to the creek again, and it looked like a bear but walked like a human!" She went on to say it just stopped and stared at her when she screamed and it made some kind of a fist-like wave before it went back down to the creek.

Well, I figured it was a resident bear, because there were a bunch of them in the rugged hills behind the folks' property. Although not all that far from town, we were the last farm on the county road before it turned to mostly a 4 x 4 trail about a mile down.

Anyway, I checked to make sure the 12 gauge was loaded; shell in the chamber and safety on, and I headed toward the bridge. When I got to the narrow bridge, I could see why the animal would have to come up from the creek and cross the road, because the spring floods had completely packed the bridge from top to bottom with brush and rubbish.

I found a set of footprints, but they were like a barefoot human would leave; only the odd thing was the tracks looked like there were four toes and no dominant, or big toe. It was loose powder dirt, so I couldn't tell for sure, but my number twelve boot fit well within the print.

I went for a ways along the creek were it wound down through the valley, and at one point I noticed a path of trampled grass where something had headed around a forested hill, and it appeared to have gone into the pines that lead into the BLM forests and mountains beyond.

I convinced Mother that it was just a bear, and warned her to just not wander too far in case it had cubs, but when Dad got home, I told him what happened. Funny thing, but he just nodded and said, "Yup, seen 'em before, but they don't bother anything 'cept now and then they steal some vegetables out of the garden, but I don't mind." He went on to say that he knew they weren't bears, but more like gorillas, but skinnier and not as stooped over, but he wasn't concerned.

So, no sense worrying Mom!

      Scott Modesto, CA

<u>Date of occurrence</u>
June, 2008

<u>Location</u>
Sunny Valley, OR

Murder in the valley: I have a farm and fairly large acreage in the Sunny Valley area north of Grants Pass, Oregon. Last fall I was walking my property, checking fences and just routine activities that come with owning rural land. I suddenly got a strange feeling that I was being watched! Not only a passing thought, but an extremely strong feeling. Looking carefully around and seeing no one, I felt uneasy enough that I returned to the house and strapped on my revolver and went back out. The feeling did not go away, so I cut short my tour and went back in the house.

About an hour later, my neighbor from up the road came up my driveway and when I went out to meet him, he said that a large cougar had been seen in our area and he was warning everyone to guard their stock. Since I don't have any ranging animals, I checked my horses and made sure the dogs were out.

The next morning I resumed my property check; knowing now that it must have been a cougar that made me feel so uneasy the day before when suddenly around the corner of my L-shaped pasture, having been alerted by two crows calling from the nearby trees, I saw a strange tan shaped object in the tall grass. It was the remains of a cougar; but it had been mutilated! I brought it back to the barn with my tractor and loaded it in my pickup and drove to the nearest Fire department which is in the town of Wolf Creek, Oregon; since there are no police in this area.

I knew the three firemen on duty and I told them I had a dead cougar, but I needed to have them look at it. The head man said, "First, before we look, was its head pulled off?" I was shocked and I answered, "Yes, its head and tail were missing when I found it, and there was blood all over!" Without so much as a pause, he responded, "You have a Sasquatch!" The other two men just nodded knowingly, and went out to confirm the condition of the big cat.

Now, I carry a gun whenever I go out on my land and so do many of my neighbors. Evidently these firemen see this kind of scene often enough that they aren't surprised by it, but I still am!

F. P.   Sunny Valley, OR

Date of occurrence
July, 2005

Location
Grayback Mountain

In July of 2005, my wife and I came up from the Bay Area to visit friends in Medford. As we usually do when we visit, we did some hiking together. Since my friend Bob is a retired forestry employee, he knows the mountains very well. This particular day, we had scheduled to hike the Grayback mountain trail at the end of Thompson Creek Rd; if I remember correctly, it was road #900. It's been a long time now, but Bob saw your article requesting submissions on Bigfoot experiences, so here's one that we'll never forget! We're sending it to you as best as I can remember.

Anyway, Bob had strained his ankle the day before, so my wife and I had to go it alone and decided to make one last hike before we returned home; we wanted to see Josephine

County's tallest mountain; so with Bob's directions, we made the trek. The road to our jump off site was rugged and rocky, and we needed our 4-wheel drive. We made it up to the beautiful meadow and stopped at the snow shelter cabin and then went out across the meadow where the Krause cabin once sat.

Just as we entered the meadow, we heard a loud howl; kind of like a mixture of a howl, a growl and a screech. It was unlike anything I have ever heard; it was kind of a grunting, groaning, almost growling. I've heard cougars scream before, but it was deeper and not at all like a coyote either! The sound lasted for almost a minute and then it abruptly stopped. My wife was unnerved, and even though I was armed, it was an uncomfortable experience. We walked past the old cabin site and just as we stood observing the mountain top above us, the sound came again from the trees above the meadow. This time we decided that it was time to go back down the trail, and we "beat feet" as they say. As we were descending the trail at a brisk pace, we heard a loud series of raps; like someone pounding a stick against a tree, but no further howls.

When we related the story to Bob, he just nodded and said, "Sorry, I forgot to mention that possibility, but I've heard similar reports from our Forest Service people over the years. Congratulations; you heard our Bigfoot!" Sorry there's not more to tell, but thanks in advance for the book.

    D. & T. Sherman San Mateo, California

Date of occurrence
October, 2011

Location
Jump Off Joe
Creek area

During deer hunting season in October 2011, I had traveled to my favorite spot by flashlight; it was around 6:45 in the morning. I was near Horse Creek off of Jump Off Joe Creek road. I will not go into more directions, because I have hunted there for years and it's a good spot; if I ever go back again!

Wanting to reach my stand before sunup, I was walking fast, but as quiet as I could. It was still dark in the canyon and the old road had puddles in the ruts. The ground was wet from the night's rain, but I wasn't making noise and it was just getting light enough that I only needed light on the path before me; when all of a sudden something moved up ahead, and I thought, "Oh no, somebody's at my spot," and I turned my light on him, but it wasn't a man! It was a tall animal with blackish-brown fur all over it and it walked hunched over; it crossed the trail and cut into a heavy stand of trees at a fast walk. I'm sure that it saw me, but it didn't seem to be running, just walking with huge steps.

It never even looked back, so I don't know what its face was like, because I kept the flashlight on it and I was so shook up I didn't even call out. It was a lot taller than my six foot three, and would probably have been close to 300 pounds or more.

I cautiously looked around the spot where the animal crossed the road, but the only thing resembling a footprint was a large flat print in a bare spot that was filling with water. I know it had to be about half again as large as my hunting boot; which means it may have been a size 14, which I've never even seen! Anyhow, I didn't see or hear anything, including a deer, and I spent about five hours on the edge of a sparse glen without even a sound, so I carefully walked out before dusk and went home.

I've never told anybody but the wife, but I quit hunting that area.

        Dave L.   Glendale, Oregon

Date of occurrence
June, 2010

Location
Rogue River Trail

My wife and I spent a fun two weeks in your area and before we returned home, we wanted to hike down your beautiful Rogue River for a ways. Our goal is to move there permanently once we are able to retire, as we have friends who live in the area.

It was just past China Gulch on our way toward Whisky Creek Cabin where the strange feelings began. It started as one of those subconscious thoughts more than anything that makes one look behind to see if someone else is following on the trail. As I looked behind me and then up at the steep slope above, my eyes met my wife's gaze as she was the first to speak; saying, "What did you see?" I answered, "Nothing, why do you ask?" She admitted to also having a feeling of being watched and she said it had begun back at the steep gully we had just passed (China Gulch), but she hadn't thought anything more of it until I started looking around.

We just assumed that there was probably a deer or some other forest dweller nearby and continued our trek. We planned to take some time to look around at Whisky Creek Cabin and camp off the trail further on. We had purposely planned our hike for early enough in the season to be well ahead of the day hikers, and having embarked from the Grave Creek boat landing, we were the only car there. For this reason, we knew there were no hikers ahead of us on the trail, but around the next bend, we saw someone in what seemed like a dark brown coat, and they cut down the sharp trail at Rainey Falls.

By the time we arrived at the trail downward, there was no one in sight. The trail downhill was wet and slick, so we decided against a stopover, but I was curious as to how this person had so quickly disappeared from sight before we arrived at the start of the steep trail downward. I was looking at the slick path for a sign of hiking boots or shoes, but all that appeared were three large depressions that were spaced far apart in the wet, slick, muddy trail; as if made by an extremely tall person. There were no signs of a tread on a sole; just fairly deep prints, and the front of each one was cut like animal claws in the front of the clearest of the three, so now we really got curious.

Our first thought was that a bear had been there earlier and that the other hiker had scared it away. Then the reality hit; if that were the case, then where were the other hiker's prints? Also, those prints were larger than the local population of black bears could make. I guessed them to be about six inches longer than my size 10 1/2 hiking boots!

Now in discussing this, my wife felt uncomfortable about

proceeding until we had satisfied our curiosity, so we carefully and quietly began a descent toward Rainey Falls; keeping a wary eye out for surprises. I was not scared, because I'm always armed with a .357 magnum revolver when hiking, just in case, but still we weren't looking for trouble, just answers. (I know that carrying a handgun in another state is taboo, but I keep it in my pack for emergencies!)

As we neared the bottom where the trail was about to become more level, we were suddenly both drawn to an area ahead where the thick brush was violently shaking and we heard a weird sound, almost like a cough or growl; and a shaking of a tall, dead snag that caused several higher branches to fragment and fly in all directions, and as we backed off, whatever it was went crashing up the almost vertical hill toward the main trail above.

We returned to the trail where we had come from and now we were faced with knowing that this thing was back on the trail between us and Whisky Creek. We had by now concluded that this was not a hiker in a brown coat, but something other, and that "other" was still in the direction we wanted to go. We chose to return to Grants Pass and head home the next day, as we didn't have anything to prove by running into what we both agreed must be a Bigfoot! We look forward to reading our story in your next book!

Matt Zachary   Redding, CA

Date of occurrence
Late Spring 2015

Location
Applegate Valley

I'm not going to tell you exactly where I was at when I experienced the fright of my life. I'm a mushroom hunter and I don't want to share my hunting grounds; this is how I supplement my husband's social security income. I've been doing this for five years now, ever since I was laid off from a job I had held for over 20 years. I sell my 'shrooms to local restaurants and small grocery stores.

I was out gathering morels, as late spring is the time to find them. I hunt alone; my husband is partially disabled and waits in the truck for me.

As it was reaching noontime, I was having success filling my mesh bags, so I stopped in a nice sunny spot for lunch. As I was eating my sandwich and apple, and enjoying the beautiful mountains around me, I started to smell a most horrible odor. I have a very good sense of smell, which makes me an excellent mushroom hunter, and this stench was just sickening.

I thought it was odd that I hadn't noticed the smell when I first sat down, and suddenly the hairs on the back of my neck were standing on end and I got that tingling sensation you get when you've just listened to a frightening story!

I quickly jumped to my feet, reaching in my pocket for my pepper spray; I'm a crack-shot with a rifle, but it's too heavy to carry. As I turned, I came face to face with the ugliest man I've ever seen; he was so hairy and seemed to be covered with dark red hair. He looked old and grizzled and his face was very wrinkled and kind of smashed in. It was then that I realized he wasn't wearing any clothes, but was covered with hair. I covered my mouth to stop myself from screaming as he reached toward me and grabbed my bags of mushrooms! I turned and ran, leaving my pack behind me; and as I got about 100 yards away, I looked over my shoulder and saw this creature was going the other way with my mushroom bags in one huge hand.

I know this story sounds crazy, and no, I hadn't been picking and sampling the wrong kind of mushrooms; but it did happen, I will swear to that. For the rest of the season, I didn't go back to that location and have found new hunting grounds. I don't think I will go back there ever again.

                Liz N.   Southern Oregon

Date of occurrence   Location
1964   Leland, OR

I'm going to tell you about a scary encounter I had when I was 18 years old. My brother Dean and I worked summers for several area loggers in the Cave Junction area. I was choke setting one day and a cable caught me and flipped me against a snag, and I got a deep gash in my thigh. It wasn't serious, but bad enough that I couldn't do heavy work for three weeks. The foreman kept me on, and I spend the days running the pickup back and forth to the hill, town and the clearcut.

One day I was heading to the shop to drop off a chainsaw for repair when I slowed down on a muddy corner on the logging road, and suddenly I saw just a glimpse out the driver's window before something smashed into the truck door so hard the truck tipped up on two wheels and I crashed into the steep dirt bank; the pickup scraped the bank and spun to the left, and stalled in the center of the road. The driver's door was jammed, so I slid over and managed to get the passenger door open and got out to see what hit me. My head had a large bump, growing by the minute, and there in the road was a huge boulder about four feet across.

Trying to figure how that huge rock came loose, I saw movement up on the hill, and in my fog, I thought it was one of our loggers, but realizing that our crew was over a mile away, I got up in the truck bed to see over the brush, and there was a giant furry beast that I at first thought was a large bear standing upright, but then it turned and disappeared behind a tree, and I watched it as it ran up the slope on two legs! It looked back at me a couple of times, and once, as I yelled at it and shook my fist, it stopped, stooped over and picked up what looked like a large tree limb and threw it toward me. Then it raised its fist and shook it, and then it disappeared!

Well, the pickup ended up with a bent frame and it took a bulldozer to remove the rock. Incidentally, the rock turned out to have been dislodged from a hole that indicated it was at least two feet in the ground; with moss on it showing it was not part of any loose earth.

My crew got quite a laugh at my expense until our foreman and the owner of the company, along with the insurance adjustor, began to believe my story when they found several large footprints where some big creature had pushed against the boulder on the hill above.

When I recovered from my wounds, I took a job on the green chain at the mill. I had no desire for a rematch!

        Chuck Campbell   Steilacoom, Washington

Date of occurrence
2004

Location
Big Bear, CA

Back in 2004 my older brother Henry had just bought a cabin up in Big Bear and had just gotten back from taken the family there for the weekend. He told that I was more than welcome to go up there with some close friends to enjoy nature. He dropped a copy of the keys in my hand, and the following weekend I headed up there with seven of my closest friends.

After late dinner we were so stuffed that we decided to go for a walk; the sky was beautiful and clear and we were all in awe of the night sky, when suddenly we heard the sound of breathing ascending from the mountain, but you could hear it so clear and it sounded so loud, not like human breathing. We all looked at each other and said, "Run!" We thought it was a bear, but the breathing was so strange and deep, like not normal by any means. We ran so fast back to the cabin and locked the door; we thought the bear was going to chase us back to the cabin and break the doors down because it was clearly running towards us, because you could hear it getting louder and louder. Thank God we never saw what it was; so just recently I was listening to Bigfoot encounters on Youtube when one of the witnesses on the show describes what she heard before she encountered a Bigfoot and her description sounded just like what we heard back in 2004 on our Big Bear weekend.

        Sincerely, Veronica Acosta   California

Date of occurrence
2009

Location
Bumping Lake, WA

A lady friend of mine and I were camping at Bumping Lake, WA when we decided to go for a walk across the dam. We heard geese honk and fly off, so I'm thinking a dog, but I didn't see any other campers.

When we got back, I'm making a fire; it's about 9 pm and as I was blowing on the fire to get it started, my friend noticed a head poking around a tree and she watched it as I blew on the fire. My friend said this thing; she called it an ape, would get excited and moved its mouth like it was blowing on the fire. All this time, she didn't say anything (she's from Utah, so not knowing about Bigfoot), and the next morning she asked me about apes in Washington state.

Well, I started looking around and tracks were everywhere and we started hearing wood knocking so we went to look

(I'm from the coast of Washington, so I know about these things), and when we got back to camp, something had taken the fish we caught and our bread; I say something, because we were the only people on the lake and the stuff was in the ice chest in the truck. Thanks for reading.

George Bossard   Yakima, Washington

<u>Date of occurrence</u># #<u>Location</u>
2011# #Oregon Caves

Please accept my request to not use my name, as I am an Oregon physician, and I don't wish to be identified, but a friend told me you were looking for stories of Sasquatch sightings and I just want to tell my story anonymously; at least it will be told.

In 2011 my wife and children and I visited the Oregon Caves. We had been there before, but this trip was to have an outing with the kids to hike the trails above and around the Chateau.

We had hiked for a couple of hours and at a particularly beautiful, scenic area, I excused myself to use nature's outdoor toilet facilities. Having trekked about 100 feet away from the family, on my return, I saw a narrow trail that wound around to my right; figuring to circle around and approach my family from a different direction, so I could jump out with a growl, like I'm prone to do, I took the trail. Well, as I came around a large tree, I almost jumped out of my skin! About fifty feet away from me was this tree that lightening or wind had toppled at one time, and just on the other side of the massive trunk was a tall, ape-looking being!

It was cautiously watching my family over the top of the still-green pine needles. It was covered with long hair, and I had an immediate mental picture of a tall Orangutan. Within less than a second, it must have sensed my presence, and it was gone! It did not even look toward me, just immediately reacted and disappeared. There was no noise, no movement, and even though I quickly pushed through the underbrush to the spot where I had seen it; nothing!

My family turned and said "We caught Dad!" When I told them what I saw, they thought it was a gag; once I convinced them I was serious, we all carefully fanned out around the tree, carefully looking for prints, hair, just anything to prove what I had seen; but no!

We all decided that it would remain a family secret; while I do believe the kids still doubt that I saw something, because on the way home I got a couple of "Really Dad's?" Anyway, it looked rather thin, about five or six feet tall with a tan, brown and orange like coat. The face was monkey like, but everything happened so fast, my impression was over in a flash. Maybe it was a youngster, since the reports I have heard always show them to have dark fur and be much taller.

A.J.   Oregon

Date of occurrence
March 2014

Location
Gin Lin Trail

The kids were ahead of us on the trail, with instructions to keep us in sight. We had hiked this area many times before as it is an excellent way to relax without worry over unsavory individuals or wild, dangerous animals. The Gin Lin area is well traveled, but we like it in early spring. Our kids are 10 and 8 years of age, so we feel comfortable in letting them lead, since the trail wraps up and around, coming out at the parking lot.

Last March, we hit a fairly warm Sunday and decided to begin our hiking season early so we could beat the tourists and maybe see signs of some wild creatures before they all went into the higher mountains for summer. At one point, about halfway around the loop, the kids suddenly disappeared from our sight. When we caught up to where we last saw them, we saw fresh tracks in the muddy loam headed away from the trail leading alongside the remnants of an old ditch that was dug to channel water from the higher slopes to feed the huge hydraulic mining operation. There are still the remains of the old control gates where the miners regulated the water flow. There, way up the slope on the edge of the ditch, we could see our two adventurers; their bright coats moving quickly along the path following the ditch. Not wanting them to fall into a hole or abandoned mine, I blew my dog (kid) whistle. They both turned, but stead of coming back, they were waving excitedly for us to join them. We quickly caught up; wanting to see what was so interesting. When we stopped, catching our breath, the kids were all excited and whispering that they had seen a monkey! They pointed to a woodsy patch beyond a couple of large felled trees where the forest was thick, and jumping up and down, they both gasped out, "It ran through that hole!"

We began to carefully climb up the slope where the kids said this animal went, and in one flat area alongside a giant root ball, we all saw very distinct footprints about as big as my wife's size 6 shoe. The thing that was different was that there were no sole or heel marks. Just a depression that looked like a bare foot, but the heels were much wider than humans would make. As we got further up the hill, the trees and brush became thicker, and suddenly, we heard what sounded like a loud, raspy cough! Then, the sound of rocks falling downhill, and after that, just a couple of sounds of falling rocks from deeper into the dark valley.

Well, we turned back, but both kids stuck to their story that they saw a long-haired monkey, but their friends laughed them into silence when they retold their story when we got home. My wife and I do believe them, and we did see the prints and heard the noises, so we can't deny the possibility.

The way the kids described it, I would say it would have been about four to five feet tall, fairly long arms, and covered with long, dark orange-brown hair.

                Neil Samson   Jacksonville, OR

Date of occurrence
July 2013

Location
Oregon Caves

Dear Sir,

We do not want our names published for the same reason that we have never before mentioned this story to anyone, because it is so preposterous for even us to believe, had it not happened so vividly!

It was on a camping trip close to the Oregon Caves. We wanted to spend a few days in one of the historic mining areas of this beautiful country, but being unfamiliar with Josephine County, we had no knowledge of just how wild it was in your vast mountains. We chose by map and word of mouth from a neighbor. Since we were tent camping, we didn't want to go too remote, so we drove the paved road

(Highway 46) south from Cave Junction and then turned right and followed several forest service roads that lead to Sucker Creek and Bolan Creek. Not too far after our turn, we spotted a turnoff that went in about a hundred feet and turned slightly around a hill which afforded us complete privacy for our campsite. Others had camped here before and there was a large rock-lined circle where they had built many campfires. We also had our propane camp stove for cooking, but since it was early in the summer, there were no fire danger warnings posted.

We had purchased two plastic gold mining pans and a couple of scoops, as we wanted to try our hands at gold panning. There were no claim signs posted, so we figured we were safe. It turned out that the water was so cold and deep, that we just spent some time digging around the steep banks and soon lost interest in freezing feet, ankles and hands, so we spent time reading and just enjoying the serenity.

We hadn't gone very far off the Caves Highway, so there was a rather steady sound of vehicles, but heavier at certain times, and since being in the forest was strange to us, it was actually comforting to hear people passing nearby.

On our second full day, we put a lunch in a backpack, took our hiking sticks and set out down the road that led deeper into the forest and toward a more remote area where the pavement ended and we were on a dirt road. We followed this road and only a couple of vehicles came by; one was a forestry pickup.

We came upon a fairly plain trail leading away from the road, so we decided to do some real exploring. I don't know how long we followed it, because originally being from Los Angeles, neither of us knew how to judge distance except by city blocks, but we must have walked for close to two hours through a beautiful area. The trail was now closed in on both sides by a gradually narrowing canyon with high, slanting sides covered by sparse trees and thick shrubs.

Suddenly we spotted a small, brown-reddish creature drinking from a pool in the stream and we thought it to be a bear cub. My husband and I had both read that you should always avoid young bears because their mothers were dangerous, so I started to back away, but he said he wanted a picture first, so he walked a little bit further and bent low and he sneaked closer with his camera. He had followed the curve in the stream which had placed him behind a large bush and I was still edging slowly away. There was a large, rocky cliff that bordered on our left and I moved to my right so I could still see Sam, when suddenly a large hairy bear-like creature appeared on a ledge; and it was carrying a huge log and walking upright on two feet. I screamed to Sam to, "Run!" but he had already seen it and started to run toward me and the huge beast had thrown the rotting log. It landed just where Sam had been and it looked like it exploded; with pieces flying all over! We both ran until we had to stop and catch our breath and that's when we realized that my husband had dropped the camera as he dove out of the way of the log.

He said he had taken one photo of the young animal which he said looked like a large orangutan, but his only view of the adult was out of the corner of his eye as he heard a noise like a growl, and as he turned, he said he glimpsed what looked like a big, shaggy ape, but standing more upright and not slumped over. It was a dark brown to orangish-brown and the baby was a lighter color. When we looked back there was no sign of either creature. We quickly hiked back to our van, packed up and left. We never returned, so our camera is likely still there!

We own a business here, so please do not publish our names. Thank you.

Name withheld   Eugene, OR

Date of occurrence
June 2015

Location
Bolan Mountain

My fiancé and I were enjoying your book *Hiking Sasquatch Country*, and since we had just moved to the area and were somewhat intimidated by the vast, mountainous areas of our new home, we found the guide quite comforting. The Southern Oregon area is very intimidating to people whose only experience with forests has been at well guided national parks, so your book gave us comfort that we weren't the only people who had ever been there.

We had already done a couple of the shorter hikes, and were now ready to spend a lot more time going deeper into the beautiful mountains. We left early on a late spring day before the tourist season began, because we wanted to explore the area at Bolan Lake. It was late enough that there were only a few small patches of snow visible, and only under the most dense areas that we drove past. When we arrived in the main area by the lake, and parked as you suggested, there was only one other set of tracks at the entrance.

We followed the trail as it climbed up and alongside the steep, rock strewn slope, ever conscious of the feeling that we were being watched! Not anything uncomfortable, but we both kept glancing up to our right, and expected to see deer or elk, or at least some animal to justify our feelings. We had thoroughly read your stories of your trips and also used Google Earth to more familiarize ourselves with the terrain. We had no trouble reaching the fire lookout, but our views were severely limited due to a cloudy haze over the mountains beneath us and toward the ocean.

We had a sandwich at a sunny spot on the way back down, sitting on a fallen tree. On our return, we took note of your reference to the cutoff to our right, which led downward to King's Saddle. The sign was on the ground, as you noted in your book, and since we had made good time, we decided to follow this trail for a ways. We had not hiked more than a half mile when we passed through a heavily forested downward curve, and there were huge piles of snow under the thick canopy, so we decided to go around one more bend and if it didn't get better, we'd head back, when all of a sudden we were assaulted by a horribly rotten smell. I can only describe it as we first felt; that something had died and was rotting, but the stench was sickening. We were so repulsed that we lost all desire to solve the mystery, and we just wanted to get away, so we turned around and beat feet back up the trail when a large chunk of wood, like a piece of log about four feet long, crashed just behind our feet with pieces striking our backs and legs!

Julie saw it first and gasped, "Look," as she pointed up the slope. My first thought was of a giant, hairy, long-legged, slumping creature. I hate to say ape, because it appeared more human-like, but without more than a two second appearance, it was more of an afterthought for both of us and just a very scary memory. Having taken advantage of our great Oregon freedom, I had secured a concealed handgun license, but I freely admit that upon seeing this creature, I had no feeling of security at all in the puny pistol in my backpack! We compared notes on our rapid retreat and we both concluded that the animal was about eight feet tall and we could only guess that due to its mass, it would weigh over 300 pounds. Neither of us really saw its ears or any feature, but were struck by its dark, red eyes!

Thanks again for the enjoyable book but in the future, we'll go later in the season!

Jerry and Julie Olsen   Medford, OR

Date of occurrence
May 2015

Location
Grayback Mountain

Tree spirits please protect me! I am an artist who carves "wood spirits" out of pine knots and I sell them at craft shows and outdoor festivals throughout Southern Oregon. This last spring, I was up on Grayback Mountain gathering my raw supplies by breaking the pine knots out of rotting, fallen trees. I knew by the signs that I was the first human to enter this remote area this year, as there were no vehicle tracks or footprints; which was normal for this isolated area anyway because it had nothing to attract people. The nearest hiking trail was about a half mile below me and it was not maintained, as I had to climb over and around downed trees before I angled away from it.

I had not been this far in before, but I found an area where the forest must have been hit with severe winds at some time past, as there were huge trees with root balls attached rotting on the ground. It was like the mother-lode of wood trolls and I began harvesting my find. I wrenched one especially large knot out of its place and raped it three times on the log to remove the loose material. Suddenly I heard three answering raps from higher up on the mountain! I was shocked, because I knew there were not possibly any people up there because there was absolutely no way in the world that anyone could be above where I was at. I pride myself on my climbing ability, and even in the summer, I could not ever climb that mountain.

Regaining my composure, I again rapped on the log the same way. Not wanting to ruin my sample, I picked up a large tree limb and used it to rap three times on the log, and almost immediately came three distinct raps echoing from above; just as before! Then I made the mistake of calling out a loud "hello!" I heard a sound like a growl and sounds like a large animal running through trees and brush. I knew as soon as it happened that calling out had been dumb, but too late! The only sound that came back was one loud crack from a ridge about eight hundred feet directly above me; then nothing but silence. I again heard a muffled sound like a snort, but that was all.

The hair on my neck tingled as I felt I was being watched and even though I have spent years tramping these forests and have heard most every deer, elk, cougar and bear, this was different. I quickly grabbed a few more knots, but now I was even more uncomfortable, so I just headed back downhill, intersected the faint trail and two hours later, I was heading down the rutted trail in four-wheel drive low range and so glad to have it!

R. H.   Applegate, OR

Date of occurrence
September 2008

Location
Galice Mining District, near the Rogue River

When a friend told me about your offer to put Bigfoot stories in print, I figured I'd finally report, what until now, I've only shared with a very few fellow miners in my district. Please do not publish my name, because I don't want people to start tromping around my claim. I go through too much work keeping it private anyway without adding to it! Thank you.

I have been a gold miner for most of 47 years now and it earns about half of my income. I also have a woodcutting and firewood business, so most of my living is earned in the outdoors. I also sell some Christmas trees during the season, so with all my outdoor knowledge, I am very used to the tracks and signs made by the local animal population.

When running my sluice, even though the work is constant, it is also boring, and I find myself to be fully familiar with the steep valley in which my gold claim sits. Seldom do I ever see humans, as my claim is not easy to get to and I have rarely invited anyone to visit, as most of us in this line of work prefer it this way. Besides, the trail to my site is rugged and I have made it even more difficult to find by adding barriers and fortifications to inhibit trespassers.

For two years now I have had visitors that have kept me on guard and sometimes at first I was afraid of a physical attack! After many close encounters, such as the occasional boulder crashing down from above; once a larger rock that must have been well over a thousand pounds, because I couldn't budge it with a five foot steel pry bar, came crashing down and landed right on top of a crudely constructed storage shed I had built on site. It destroyed the small building, crushed two fuel cans, and scattered a two month's supply of food staples into the creek.

I was in the creek when this happened, and my reaction was to grab my revolver (which I constantly wear) and I quickly fired several shots up the slope where the rock came from. After I had reloaded my gun, I changed out of my rubber boots; and in hiking shoes, I climbed the steep slope, grabbing and grasping bushes, shrubs and trees, following the skid trail until I located the source from where the huge rock had lain. The hole where this rock had come from was a depression that was over a foot and a half deep. I don't know three men that together could have dislodged that rock!

I searched for signs of a pry mark or sign of boots, and there was a print in the wet soil where the boulder had been that looked like a huge, bare human foot print, but yet, it was wider. It was about as long as my size eleven boot print, and when I placed my boot over it, the print was slightly longer and twice as wide. The toes looked similar to a human, but the ends of the toes seemed to be broken as if they had large claws that broke the soil at the tips of the imprint.

I'll admit that when it happened, I was angry, thinking that somebody had tried to kill me and wreck my camp; I realized that this was not a human. I got over my anger and was able to understand that I myself was the trespasser!

That event happened about September of 2008 and since then, I have several times caught a glimpse of what appears to be two individual dark brown creatures; never together, but each sighting was at a time when I was moving some equipment or unclogging a blocked waterway, and they appeared to be just observing. One seems to be substantially larger and a darker brown, and the smaller one is a lighter brown, and I suppose if standing straight, would be about six feet; where the larger one would be about eight feet or more.

I have never heard a growl, but over the last two years, I have many times heard loud squeals on occasion, and quite often, I hear sounds like a stick banging against a tree, and even more often, a louder sound like a large branch being banged against a hollow tree or log. Then another similar sound answers from somewhere else.

>R. J……Galice Mining District

Date of occurrence	Location
Unknown	Gold Eye Lake, Alberta, Canada

When I was camping at Gold Eye Lake, Alberta (near Nordegg) I meditated one day after supper, and after a while, heard a foot stomp a couple of times and then a whistle. It was along a "cut line". Also, when I did my Qi Gong exercises in the mornings it was quiet and it felt like nature was watching me.

I didn't actually see anything, but it was more of a feeling. Thinking back upon the incident, I believe there was a "forest human" out there watching me and wondering what I was doing.

Wendy Starr   Red Deer, Alberta

Date of occurrence
June 2014

Location
Sturgis Fork Trail

I've been following your Facebook page for a while now and I just saw your post about having space for a few more Bigfoot stories. I've never told this story to anyone other than a couple of close friends, but have decided to share it with you.

I've hiked all over Southern Oregon, and even though I'd been on Grayback Mountain before, I hadn't taken the Sturgis Fork Trail before. It's a rough old road, but once I traded in my Subaru for a Jeep Wrangler, I figured I'd finally be able to make it to the trail head.

Early one summer morning my dogs and I set out for a day of hiking. I have two Bullmastiffs. People always tell me I shouldn't hike alone, but I feel safe with my two kids. The male, his name is Brutus and he weighs about 150 pounds. My little girl, Annie, is smaller at 100 pounds. I carry my water and lunch for all of us, while Brutus carries some extra water in his saddle bags.

We were the only vehicle there when we arrived at the trail head; I wasn't surprised as this is not a very well-known hiking area. As we started out, we passed several marked gold claims; the creek was running over the banks some, so the trail was a bit muddy. It was there that I first noticed two sets of prints. They were quite odd; they weren't boot or shoe prints, but looked like those Vibram shoes that have an individual slot for each toe. One set was very large, maybe three times the size of my ladies size 6, and the other looked like a man's size 14. I didn't think that type of shoe would be good for hiking, but then I've seen people hiking in sandals.

Bullmastiffs are excellent trackers and were anxious to start following the footsteps. We continued on up the trail and came upon a lovely meadow. The flowers were just starting to bloom and it was almost breathtaking. I would have liked to pause a bit longer, and although my dogs are well-trained and normally very obedient, they were very keen to keep going. As we neared a rocky outcropping, we came across a dead deer just off the trail. I should say the front half of a deer, as the hindquarters were missing. Now Brutus and Annie were getting very excited as I started looking around for what might have killed this deer since it was obviously a fresh kill, for the blood was still freely flowing. We continued on, perhaps fool-hardily, to the rocky outcropping. It looked like it would have been an ideal spot for a bear to hibernate, but I didn't see any signs of bear or any other predator.

As I stood there debating whether to go on or not, the wind changed direction and we all got a good whiff of a strong animal smell; it was a cross between the scent of an animal and a human with horrible body odor. I decided it was time for us to get back to the Jeep and find a different place to hike when Brutus tugged so hard I couldn't keep hold of his leash. He dashed up the trail, while I was yelling for him to come back and Annie was starting to wail. Now I was faced with having to decide to follow him or wait for him to return; there was no way I was going to leave him there! It wasn't long before the decision was made for me, as I started to hear a loud, pounding noise. It sounded like someone was hitting a tree with a bat. It was in a set of three and then I heard another set of pounding coming from much farther away. Annie and I started running up the trail, and I'm blowing on the whistle I carry around my neck. As we rounded the curve, we almost got run over by Brutus running toward us. He stopped long enough to bark at me and then continued down the trail. After a several yards he turned to make sure we were following. He must have decided we weren't quick enough and came back to encourage us to follow him.

Now Bullmastiff's are loyal and very protective of their humans, so I followed his lead and we ran as fast as we could back to the Jeep. When we got there, Brutus was just shaking like a leaf and crying to get inside the vehicle. I unlocked the door and we all jumped in; not bothering to remove our packs or stop and catch our breaths.

Once we were back on Thompson Creek Road, I found a place to pull over. Brutus was still shaking, but starting to calm down, so we got out; I stowed our packs in the back and got the dogs and myself some water. We didn't go hiking that day, but stopped at a nice county park to relax a bit before heading home. I don't know what was there on the mountain, but it was scary enough to make a courageous and fierce dog back down!

        Jane Evans   Josephine County, Oregon

Date of occurrence
May 2005

Location
near the old
McCaleb Ranch

My friend Duane and I drove through Selma, OR and made the turn that took us to the McCaleb Ranch which is now a Boy Scout camp. We parked in the area up above, because I didn't know if the floating bridge was safe to drive over and also because we are not scouts. I didn't see any sign of people at the big log house they have.

We walked down the path and across the swinging bridge. We had to hold on because there was melting ice on the bridge, and the sun hadn't melted it off yet. When we got across the bridge, we turned left and went up river to check out our old deer hunting spot to plan ahead for the next fall, and to kind of scout for a good place to come out and camp a few times that summer. I think we probably had got about two miles back off the river and close to a deep, brushy ravine that had water too deep to cross that ran into the Illinois River, so we had just followed it away from the river.

We sat down for lunch at a kind of brushy area next to a deep gully coming down the mountain behind us, and after a snack, I took out my Iver Johnson .22 revolver and took a shot at a white rock on the hillside, and all of a sudden, all hell broke loose! This giant bear looking thing jumped up from across the river and let out a screech and growl of some sort as it was coming at us. He was huge, and Duane said, "Run!"

I knew I didn't want to stand there with my .22 to fight a bear, so I took off behind Duane through the tall brush. I think we both must have fallen down a couple of times, but we ran steady 'til we saw the Illinois River again, and as we got up to the higher ground, we both realized that we were not being followed. I've never run so fast in all my life. Duane lost his backpack and his scout knife, and I had dropped my canteen and lost my cap, but we were still shaking!

I am not embarrassed to say that we were both really scared. After we made it back across the bridge was the first time we slowed down; just in case! Comparing notes, we figured it couldn't have been a bear because it ran on its back feet. Before it stood up to chase us, it must have been on all fours, but thinking back, we agreed it had to be a lot more than seven feet, and it had dark brownish hair all over it, kind of a squished face, a baboon like nose, but much shorter and wider. Its mitts were really huge and neither of us can remember seeing its feet.

We never went back and never hunted there again, but my dad said it might have been an old gold miner, but both of us knew that no man could be that big or move as fast as it did when it came after us!

                T. L.   Cave Junction, OR

Date of occurrence
September 2004

Location
near Jeffrey Pine Loop

Hi, we have your book and when we saw your note on the Sasquatch Watch page for stories for another book, my wife wanted me to tell you about our personal experience. It happened back in late September of 2004 on the Eight Dollar Road about where you describe the Jeffrey Pine Loop, but I don't remember that even being there. We had been as far as the bridge, and then drove back toward the highway and decided it would be fun to just walk down the hill to the Illinois River. With the road on one side and the river on the other, my wife was comfortable that I wouldn't get us lost like I've done before. Anyway, we parked on a short cutoff that was just off the road and found a deer trail down the slope toward the river.

When we got to the river, there was a well-used trail that went both ways. We decided to turn left, because that part seemed less traveled and it curved farther away from the road, so we hoped to see some deer or a coyote. We were walking quiet like and not talking when we heard a splashing sound that we both thought was just the rapids, but then it stopped, and a minute later it started up again. All of a sudden, off to our right, there was a big brown bear crossing the river, but it turned out it wasn't! It was the top of a critter that looked like a big hairy ape, but it was walking on the bottom of the river, and when it came out it was on two feet. It looked back at us and made a loud kind of "woof" sound; only it did it three or four times in a row. Its face as we could see, looked kind of like an old, wrinkly man with big ears, but it only looked at us for a minute, and we were about two hundred feet away. Then it hit shore and headed around the curve, but there wasn't much brush, just real short stuff, so we must of seen it for another couple of minutes. It glanced back once and then again, and then it kind of shook its arms like it was made, and my wife said she thought it looked like steam or spit came out of its mouth, but the river noise covered any sound. Then it just jumped about a foot with both feet in the air and stomped down; like a person when they are real mad and then the darn thing jumped over a log and disappeared! It's hard to judge how big it was because the river was too deep for us to wade; not that you could have paid us to do it anyway, but we'd think maybe six feet tall.

My wife called the forestry office when we got home, but they just seemed like it was a normal thing, so outside of a few friends, we just let it be until we saw your note. We look forward to seeing our story in your new book. Please send it to the enclosed address, but we prefer our names to be kept private.

     Anonymous Grants Pass, Oregon

Date of occurrence
1999

Location
Applegate Valley

Dear Sir,

Please consider our story for your book. Back about 1999, we had a strange visitor at our place. We live a ways out in the Applegate, in the Thompson Creek area, and that's as close as I will give, as we are private people. A friend in town who has a computer connection told us you were writing a book and he remembered our scary experience and told us to write it out and he'd sent it to you off his machine; so here you are and please don't tell where we live. Thank you, (name withheld).

Our dogs had taken to barking for quite a few days, like they do if a cougar or bear comes around, but this started happening every night just about dark in the fields and when it was already dark in the woods. My husband had taken the shotgun and gone out where our dogs were barking for about the fourth night in a row, and when he got to where they were, he found one of them dead alongside a small blacktail deer, but he said it really shook him up, because the deer was almost broken in half and its spine and ribs were sticking out. Our dog Maverick, who weighed about a hundred pounds, had its head missing. My husband said he looked around but couldn't find it, and he was too shook up to look any more, so he brought him home and buried him.

That was a really sad time for us and my husband was really mad. He thought it had been a cougar, so he took the deer and hoisted it up on a tree limb where he could see it from the barn. The next night he snuck out to the barn and locked the dogs inside and then he just sat back in the hay mow so he was in the dark but where he could see and not be seen. He had his 30.06 rifle with him. All of a sudden around dusk, the dogs started yapping real loud and he could hear them scratching to get out, but the windows were too high. The deer was in a tree about a 150 feet from the barn and my husband said he had his rifle ready; and all of a sudden he smelled something really rotten and he thought he was smelling the deer; when this dark brown ape-man critter appeared alongside the tree. It reached toward the deer just as my man pulled the trigger. He jerked it, out of being nervous, and the bullet tore into the tree and the ape-man disappeared. He let the dogs out and they made a beeline right past the deer and up the hill, and he said he could hear them barking and howling until he couldn't hear them anymore.

It was about three hours later when they finally came home. One had a broken paw and the other two each had a couple of deep gashes in their necks and side, and one had a torn lip, but they survived. We never again had another experience with this animal. My husband said it was about seven or eight feet high as he measured where its head showed by the tree branches, and it had really long arms, big paws and the imprints its feet left, he said were bigger than his rubber barn boots, so that he guessed would make it about a size 16 or more!

Please keep our names private, because people don't need to think we're nuts out here in the country! Please send our book to (address withheld).

Anonymous   Applegate Valley

Date of occurrence
August, 2011

Location
Shan Creek Overlook

I'm not sure what we saw this day and we think it was a Sasquatch, but I guess we'll never really know. Almost five years ago on a hot summer day, three friends and I decided to hike up to the Onion Mountain fire lookout tower. We decided to make a day of it, so we packed a lunch and plenty of sodas and water. There was a lot of haze in the air once we reached the tower, so we didn't have a great view of the far away mountains, but we sat up on the tower and had our lunch. On the way back down the mountain, my friend Mary got all excited and said she just spotted a metallic blue snake. I quickly looked where she was pointing and glimpsed the bright blue tail quickly moving away. I laughed and told her that is was just a skink. Mary had just moved to Grants Pass from Portland and said the only place she had ever seen a snake was at a zoo. I told her a skink was a type of lizard and had four legs. This got the four of us talking about snakes, and Bill mentioned that on our way back to town we could stop at the Shan Creek Overlook where you can almost always spot a snake or two; sometimes even a rattlesnake. So that's what we did.

We parked in a small turnout across the road from the overlook, carefully watching the ground for snakes. Just before we reached the area where you can look out over the valley, we heard a loud screaming sound. As we ran toward the precipice, we could see the tops of the trees below us furiously shaking. As we looked over the edge the noise suddenly stopped and the trees stopped moving. We stood there for a few minutes talking about what it might have been. We thought maybe a cougar had caught a rabbit or even a deer. That's when the pounding started. It sounded like a club being hit against a tree right below us, and then we heard more pounding from farther away. Next we heard the sound of something climbing up towards us; Bill said "Run!" We all ran as fast as we could back to the car, jumped in and got out of there. We stopped at Griffith Park before going back to town to talk about what had happened. We had all heard stories about Bigfoots living behind the Oregon Caves and we concluded that this is what it must have been.

The four of us; Mary, Bill, Ellen and I never talked about this again until this past Christmas. I came home for a visit, I'm in school at Boise State, and the four of us got together to talk about old times. Bill brought up our adventure, and after discussing it for a little while, we decided we'd send you the story as long as you don't use our last names.

    Bill, Ellen, Mary and Jack   Grants Pass, Oregon

Date of occurrence
July, 2000

Location
Tucker Flat
Campground

My encounter with what I still believe to be a Sasquatch happened almost sixteen years ago. One of my friends had won a permit to raft the wild and scenic portion of the Rogue River, so he and three other experienced rafters were making plans to raft from Grave Creek to Illahe, a trip of about 40 miles. Knowing I didn't like to raft, they asked me if I would be willing to meet them at several points along the way to refresh their supplies and drive them back to the Grave Creek boat ramp when they were done. I readily agreed, thinking it would give me plenty of time to do some hiking and camping.

When we met at the boat ramp to begin our separate trips, it was agreed that I would meet them at Tucker Flat Campground in two days, as they wanted to stop and spend the first night at Winkle Bar; the site of the author Zane Grey's old cabin. After helping my buddies get their supplies loaded in their raft, I waved goodbye, jumped in my truck and headed for Tucker Flat.

As you know, the Marial Road is not the easiest route to travel on, and I soon realized I had a flat tire. I stopped to put my spare on, and it took me quite some time as I had difficulty removing the lug nuts. It was late afternoon when I pulled into the campground, so I quickly pitched my tent and set about making some dinner. I noticed there were two other tents already set up in the campground, but their occupants were nowhere to be seen. After dinner, I packed all my foodstuffs into the bear-proof locker that's in the bed of my truck. This area is known for its large bear population, so I always take this precaution. It was about 9:00 when I decided to turn in. I got settled in my tent with a lantern and a great book; it has no bearing on my story, but coincidentally it was "Rogue River Feud" by Zane Grey.

I read for a couple of hours and I had just turned out my light when the ruckus started. It began with the sound of heavy footsteps, and at first I assumed it was people just coming back to their tents. Suddenly I heard something breathing right outside of my tent, and when I took a peak out the screen, and with a full moon out, I saw what looked like an extremely large bear standing up on its hind legs, and whatever it was began to growl and moan! Then it started pulling at my tent and dragging it away with me still inside; I kept absolutely still and silent. After several minutes it moved off, and then I heard it thrashing around the area where the other tents were. I quietly got out of my tent, and in a crouching run, got over to my pickup and climbed in. After I was safely inside, I started it up and turned my headlights on which were shining in the same direction the noises were still coming from. This beast was huge, and it certainly wasn't a bear. It stopped destroying the other tents and looked towards me; it bared its teeth and started walking toward me. I threw the gearshift in reverse and backed out of my campsite as quickly as I dared! Once I reached the road, the beast was still in my headlights; it just stood there for a second and then turned back toward the woods. I quickly drove over to the Marial Lodge and spent the night in my truck in their parking lot, as they were full-up for the night.

The next morning I was able to make arrangements to stay at the Lodge for the next night and made arrangements for my rafters to stay when they arrived the next day. When my friends arrived I did not say a word about what had happened and simply told them I wanted to treat them to a comfortable night's lodging before they got back on the river. Except for meeting my friends down at the river, I did not leave the lodge.

After an uneventful night, the rafters got back in the water planning to spend the night at Camp Tacoma and then the next day they would land at the Illahe campground. I headed to Grants Pass to find myself a new tent and then headed for Agness over Bear Camp Road. I spent that night at the Singing Springs Resort; I was now uneasy about camping alone. The next morning, I arrived at the Illahe campground in time to set up everyone's tents and I was comforted by the fact that the campground was almost full. When my friends arrived just after noon, I was more than happy to let them tell me all about their trip; they had a great time.

To this day, I have not shared my story with anyone, nor have I returned to Tucker Flat campground or the Marial Lodge. The creature, which I know was a Sasquatch, stood at least 7 feet tall and had very dark reddish-brown hair; I think its eyes were an amber color, but my light may have distorted that.

James Moore   Grants Pass, Oregon

Date of occurrence
July, 1996

Location
Siskiyou National Forest

I have been a U.S. Forest Service ranger for 22 years and have spent a lot of my time in the Siskiyou National Forest on the border of California and Oregon. I have often repeated my story to co-workers and close friends, and a friend told me you wanted true experiences; so here you are.

My BLM partner and I were working out of Happy Camp, California. The entire area of Happy Camp is rich in gold mining history and tales of Sasquatch run rampant throughout these mountains. We who live and work in this region accept these stories as they are, as the storytellers are so adamant about their experiences and there are so very many. All of these encounters are so similar that we who work for the government offices in the area remain neutral.

After all, if these creatures are real, then we have a duty to protect them too.

My BLM partner was charged with cruising the mountainous area between Happy Camp and the Oregon border; I was assigned to help. Our objective was to conduct a feasibility study for timber thinning and fire danger. We drove the forestry road along the border which runs just south of Bolan Lake and camped two days in the hills. The first night we heard what sounded like footsteps in the forest downhill from our tent, but chocked it up to deer. After settling exhausted into the tent on day two, it happened!

We had camped close to a creek that flowed south into a small unnamed slough. Falling asleep almost immediately, my partner and I were awakened just after midnight by footsteps close to the tent. First there was the sound of snapping of twigs and then something hit the tent hard enough to cause our florescent battery light to fall from the tent pole and crash on the ground. We both bolted out of the tent with flashlights in hand. We ran around each side of the tent scanning the dense forest all around and down the steep slope behind the tent. We both heard something crashing and thumping ahead of us, and finally the going became too impassable. We made our way back up to the tent and found a large piece of pine tree limb, about four inches across, that had hit our tent hard enough to tear the fabric where the screen window was attached. The limb was over five feet long and looked like it was a large hiking stick. There were no trees within 30 feet, and with no wind, so we knew it had been thrown! We were wide awake yet, when about 20 minutes later we heard a scream! It was loud and sounded human! The scream came again several minutes later and it was followed by a kind of growling and grunting, and then several more loud, long lasting screams came again over the next hour and a half. Whatever it was seemed like an out of control human just raging in anger.

When dawn came, we lit out as fast as we could; survey over! Our friends have all heard about our experience, and strangely, no one laughed or even questioned our nightmare, because these tales are heard so often, everyone just nods in understanding. Due to our government rules, I must remain anonymous, so just call me Red; my friends will know who wrote this; it's my true story; every word!

                Red

We are pleased to have two submissions from "Doc" Bashford. Doc moved to Oregon from Ohio and is well respected in the Bigfoot Hunters community.

Many of us remember when Doc owned the "Bigfoot Cavern" in Kerby, Oregon. He had a nine foot tall carved wood Sasquatch just inside the door. This famous landmark dates back to the early days of Oregon's logging and mining, and the building is entirely built of stone. The floor still bears the holes made by the loggers' hobnail boots as they stopped in after work. Doc and his partner featured great food and a full bar with live music. A whole wall was filled with plaster casts of Bigfoot prints and newspaper articles of Doc's exploits and memorabilia.

Doc is travelling now, but we look forward to more input from him in the future. Thanks Doc!

Date of occurrence
August 1977

Location
Southern Ohio

The nearest town to this encounter is Minford in Scioto County. It was approximately 10:30 p.m. on a clear night. My grandma was on the phone with a church friend and my grandpa was out doing something related to school. I stepped out onto the back porch to get some guitar strings I had left in the car which was parked in the short drive way. As soon as I stepped outside I noticed a very foul smell; like skunk and rotten meat. It was a very weird odor, unlike anything I had smelled before.

I reached down and picked up a broken axe handle and started tapping it on the concrete as I walked, as I wasn't interested in running into a skunk. I proceeded to the rear of the car and started to put the keys in the lock. I heard a rattling sound that seemed to be coming from everywhere. I stopped and looked around, and suddenly there was silence. That struck me as odd because the pond behind the house was normally raging with crickets and frogs, but it was absolutely silent.

I again went for the lock, and again the rattling sound started. It was clear, but I saw nothing. Then I realized I was being watched from behind.

As I turned, the rattling sound returned, and there 30 or 40 feet away was a huge creature at least eight feet tall. It had no neck, very long arms and was reddish black in color. The beast was covered from head to toe with hair which was longer on its forearms and around where its neck should have been. Its face was hairless around its mouth, eyes and nose. It had a heavy brow and I could not see its eye color. Its arms swung forward and hit the barbed wire fence it was standing behind; that was the rattling sound. I have no idea of how long I stood there in shock!

I hit the kitchen table on my way through the house, and my grandma said I was making no sense as I ran down the hall to my room. My gun cabinet was locked, so I began breaking the glass front as Grandma came in telling me to calm down. I told her there was a monster outside. She said it's one of your friends playing a joke and if you take that gun out I will call the sheriff. I told her to call the sheriff, game warden and state police. I zipped past her carrying my loaded 30/30; she followed right behind me. I ran out of the house and the thing was gone. She asked me where is this monster and what on earth is that smell? I kept telling her it was right there. After saying that a couple of times, we both heard something going through the trees beside the house back towards the fence. Then the entire fence line shook, and there it was, running through the field and up the hill which was void of trees until you get to the top.

My gun was sighted on it. It was amazingly fast, and I kept saying it runs like a man. I don't know if I was saying it aloud or not, but something in my head said, "What if?" But it's way too big and no man can run like that uphill; I lowered the gun as it got to the top. It turned and screamed at us. It started out low pitched and then went up very high; it lasted for maybe 8 to 10 seconds, then it walked into the woods.

The thing scared the bejeebies out of Grandma. I've told very few people this story because they just laughed. I've always told myself, "One day I will bring whatever it was in. Then we'll see who is nuts."

Edward "Doc" Bashford   formerly of Kerby, Oregon

<u>Date of occurrence</u>
November 2009

<u>Location</u>
Smith River area,
Northern California

This happened early in November of 2009 when I was living in Kerby, Oregon. I got a call from a ranger friend of mine whom I had met many times before in the area. He asked if I wanted to go with him on a hike, looking for bear hunters or maybe evidence of illegal trapping or hunting taking place. I gladly accepted, as I am always ready to support our law enforcement officers.

We crossed at Patrick Creek and headed south. Since he knew about my searches for the elusive Sasquatch, all I heard for an hour and 45 minutes was, how long he has been in these forests and there is no such thing as Bigfoot; it was just in my imagination. We came up on a ridge that had a place where we could see the valley below. I had my binoculars and I was scanning the valley. There below us were three creatures about a quarter mile distant in a grassy area by the edge of a cliff. I had to laugh. He asked what was so funny? I pointed and said, "Right down there is my imagination." He looked; his words were, "Holy shit, you gotta be kidding me" etc.

The male stood erect facing us as if he could see us. The female had breasts and was doing something in the grass with a much smaller creature. The big guy stood still. We watched them for at least 10 minutes. Then the big guy, (my rough guess is he was about eight feet tall) did something with his right hand. They stood, got in a single file line and turned, and went into the tree line along the cliff which was above them. Then they were gone!

The ranger, I will call him Scott to protect his identity, was very nervous and actually in a panic; he had been a ranger for 15 years and never saw anything like that. I insisted we go down there. We did, although it took us a while. You could see where they had been and Scott was now paranoid. We followed the trail; they went in along the cliff and after about 45 yards they went up the cliff. Straight up, so we did also. Trust me, he didn't want to, and it took about 45 minutes to get to the top. We tracked them west along the edge of the cliff and then to my surprise, they went straight back down. They left us sitting with now miles between us. He even said, "Wow that was smart," which made him more paranoid. Well it was getting dark and I had no night gear with me, so I wasn't gonna talk him into going farther anyhow.

He never said a word on the four mile track back to the river but was very scared. We said our goodbyes and when I called him the next day; he said he had turned in his resignation. Scott now lives in Santa Barbara. I guess the scare was enough to cause him to leave our wilderness!

Edward "Doc" Bashford   formerly of Kerby, Oregon

ALL THE BELLS AND WHISTLES
(A GUIDE TO HIKING OUR AREA)

Be aware of bears and cougars when hiking in our beautiful wilderness. Our gorgeous country is home to many creatures that could hurt or kill the unwary. Rattlesnakes are possible to encounter, but are seldom a bother. You are most likely to encounter them if you are hiking at dusk. Black bears are plentiful, as well as our cougar population, which is growing. Bears are most dangerous when surprised, and if you should come between a mother and her cubs, you could be in big trouble! Cougars are really becoming more abundant, and have been known to stalk, and occasionally, but rarely attack hikers, and I don't recall any attacks in Oregon.

Being a noisy hiker is not conducive to getting prize wildlife photos. I never worry, because our dogs usually create enough commotion by getting their leashes tangled and crashing around; but hikers are advised to be aware of animal signs, and if you have an encounter, just back away.

Here's where having all the "Bells and Whistles" comes in handy. Hikers are advised to be cautious around rivers and streams, and not to reach into holes without first probing with a stick, although rattlers will normally sense vibration and move off. Hikers concerned with cougars and bears can always do as the Alaskans, and wear small bells and carry a whistle.

Bears and cougars oftentimes use the same trails we do, and being able to recognize their "scat" is helpful. Bear droppings normally contain berries and animal fur.

Cougar scat will contain animal fur, and also small "bells and whistles." Just kidding, have a great time!

Be prepared by bringing plenty of water for each member of your party. You should also bring some extra high energy snacks, a first aid kit, and yes, a whistle. It's not a good idea to hike alone in this rugged country. If you are hiking with dogs, don't forget to bring plenty water and high energy snacks for them as well.

Know where you are going, and make sure someone else knows where you are going to be and when you plan to return. Be sure to have a good map of the area, because you cannot always rely on GPS systems. People have died in our wilderness area by trusting only their GPS as our mountains can affect their functioning.

Respect the environment, whatever you pack in; make sure you take it back out. You will not find any trash barrels or bathroom facilities along the way!

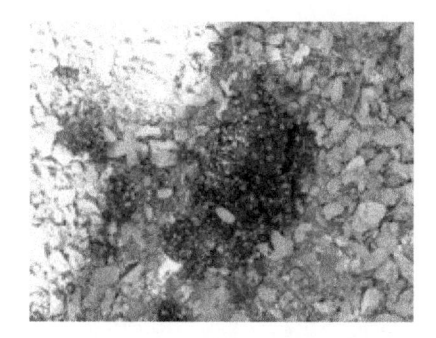

ABOUT THE AUTHORS

Gary and Wendy Swanson have lived in Grants Pass, Oregon for the last eight years, where they have enjoyed hiking throughout the spring, summer and fall months with their dogs. In addition to their love of hiking, they also enjoy history. Southern Oregon is full of history of gold mining, logging and fishing along the wild and scenic Rogue River; so for them, it has been a great place to research history, explore the countryside and hike all at the same time.